Read-Together Bible Stories

Text by Christina Goodings
Illustrations copyright © 2015 Jimothy Oliver
This edition copyright © 2015 Lion Hudson

Published by Lion Children's Books
an imprint of
Lion Hudson plc
Wilkinson House, Jordan Hill Road,
Oxford OX2 8DR, England
www.lionhudson.com/lionchildrens

ISBN 978 0 7459 6544 4

First edition 2015

A catalogue record for this book is available from the British Library

Printed and bound in China, June 2016, LH06

Read-Together
BIBLE STORIES

Retold by Christina Goodings

Illustrated by Jimothy Oliver

LION
CHILDREN'S

Contents

Noah 6
Genesis 6-9

Joshua 18
Joshua 6

David 26
1 Samuel 17

Jonah 36
Jonah 1-4

Daniel 46
Daniel 6

Baby Jesus   56
Matthew 1-2; Luke 1-2

The storm at sea   64
Matthew 8; Mark 4; Luke 8

The hole in the roof   72
Matthew 9; Mark 2; Luke 5

The good Samaritan   80
Luke 10

The lost sheep   90
Matthew 18; Luke 15

Noah

NOAH LOOKED AT the sign.

"To the sea" it read.

He folded his arms. Yes, he was building a boat a long way from the sea. And he wasn't going to give in to any bullying about it.

A stone flew over toward him.

"Loser," came a shout. It was one of the young men standing by his boat-in-progress. Some of the others were having a go at vandalizing the gangplank.

"Oi, you lot. Clear off!" shouted Noah.

"Is your big Mr God going to get us if we don't?" mocked one of them.

"Probably," said Noah calmly. "In fact, if you go on fighting and squabbling, the answer is 'definitely'."

"Ooooooh, SCAAARY,"

teased the young men. But they all trooped off.

Noah went up to the boat and fixed the gangplank.

From over the hill came his wife and three daughters-in-law. They had an ox cart full of supplies.

From out of the wood came his three sons, driving some of the farm animals.

"All aboard!" called Noah.

Then came the animals, two by two, as if called by God from the fields and forests.

What a racket!

cluck

cluck

"Come on," said Noah. "God is going to flood the world and all its wickedness."

mooooooooooooo

rraaahh

squeak

When Noah and his family and all the animals were safe
on the ark, the rain came, and the flood rose.

Days became weeks.
Weeks became months.

The floodwaters lapped
against the side of the boat.

Then one day...

The ark bumped into a mountaintop.
Slowly, slowly, the water trickled away.
The mountaintops looked like islands.

Noah sent a raven to look for land, but it flew away.

Noah sent out a dove instead. The second time he did so, the dove came back with a twig in its beak.

"Great news!" cried Noah. "Somewhere there's proper dry land. The plants are growing green again."

Then, at long last, the flood was over.
A rainbow spread across the sky.

"Everyone out!"

called Noah.
"It's time to start the world again. And this time, let's get it right.

"You animals can have young and fill the earth again.

"Mrs Noah, you can have a new vegetable garden, and I'll get these young people busy with the farm again."

Quietly, God spoke. "Remember this whenever you see
a rainbow. Never again will I wipe out the world with a
flood. There will be summer and winter, seedtime and
harvest for ever."

Joshua

JOSHUA LOOKED UP at the walls of Jericho. They were high.
They were strong. And they had spiky bits around the top.
  But the spiky bits weren't part of the walls. They were
the spears of the soldiers who were standing on guard
behind the battlements.

"Troublesome," said Joshua to himself. How was he going to lead his people into Canaan, as God wanted, if he had to get past Jericho? Clearly, the people of Jericho weren't about to welcome newcomers.

Then he heard God speaking:

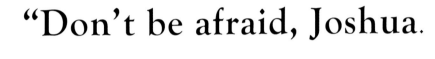

"Don't be afraid, Joshua.

Don't give up hope.

"Obey my laws and follow my instructions. Then I will always be with you to help you."

"OK," said Joshua, in a very tiny voice.

God's instructions were not the usual battle plan.

"God wants me to line up a big parade," announced Joshua. "First, seven priests, each with a trumpet.

"And DON'T blow until I say," he added to the priests.

"Then, more priests carrying the golden ark of the covenant.

"Take care not to touch the box itself," he told the carriers. "It's holy. Inside are the stones on which the laws of our people are written. They are God's laws, which tell us what is right and what is wrong.

"And then the soldiers," Joshua finished.

"We don't have great weapons," the soldiers complained. "We've been wandering in the desert for years. All our stuff is a bit worn out."

"No problem," Joshua replied. "This is God's plan. Watch... and wonder!"

When everyone was ready, Joshua ordered the big parade to march around Jericho.

"NOW for the trumpets," cried Joshua. "Everyone else... shhhhhh."

He did the same the next day, and the next, and the one after that and the one after that again and...

"Let's see. We've marched 1, 2, 3, 4, 5 days," muttered a soldier. "Are we going to do the same again?"

"We are," said his friend.

"The soldiers guarding Jericho must be thinking we're totally weird," said the first.

"Then they'll be scared," said the friend.

"Or scornful," said the first. "Anyway, day six, here we come. Same as before, of course."

On the seventh day, Joshua had new instructions.

"Today we march around seven times. When I give the signal, the trumpeters will give a great blast of noise.

"You fighters: shout at the top of your voices."

The city walls fell down. All the spiky spears and the soldiers holding them tumbled in a heap. Joshua and his soldiers took the city.

David

DAVID WAS HAVING a big day out. He had his shepherd's stick and his shepherd's sling, but he wasn't looking after the sheep today. No, much more fun: his father had told him to take a basket of food to his brothers in the army.

As he came close to the army camp...

RRRRAAAAAAGH *aagh aagh aagh*

The army's blood-curdling battle cry echoed around the hills.

And then came an answering voice – louder, deeper, scarier.

raoooooooooooooooh

David scampered along to see.

Then he rushed to find his brothers.

"Did I miss the fight? Are you going to win? Will you win if you have some homemade cheese first?" David asked, somewhat breathlessly.

"Just look over there," said his eldest brother, with a bit of a sneer. "Those Philistines have got a giant fighting on their side."

"That's Goliath," said his second eldest brother. "If anyone can beat him, we win the war. But it has to be single combat."

"No fear," said the third eldest. "Not even for the big reward King Saul has offered."

"I'll go," said David. "I've got my sling. Dad warned me to take care against those Philistine rascals."

"Cheeky brat," replied all three.

"I'll go and ask King Saul then," said David sulkily.

News of David's plan reached Saul before David did. For a few minutes he actually began to hope that he might have found someone to fight Goliath.

Then in came David.

"Oh," said Saul. "You're a boy.

"It's a kind and brave offer you've made, and one day I'm sure you'll be a great fighter. But I'm not letting you go off and get killed.

"For one thing, what ever would I say to your mother?"

"But I can fight – I CAN," said David. "Look, I'm a shepherd boy. I've killed lions and bears that came prowling. I can hit anything.

"And anyway, our God is better than the Philistine gods. So I'm BOUND to win."

Saul leaned forward.

"Listen," he said. "Just try on my armour. See if you feel like fighting once you're wearing that."

David tried on the armour. He couldn't move.

"No, I don't," he said. "I'll go as I am."

THUD

To the amazement of Saul and the entire Israelite army, David set off down the slope toward Goliath.

At the stream that ran in the valley, he stopped to pick up five stones.

Then he walked up the next hill to face the giant.

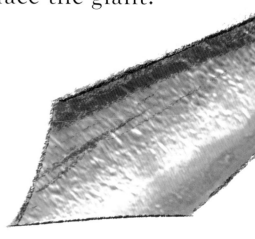

"Do you think I'm a DOG, coming to fight with your stick?" roared Goliath.

"No, I don't," replied David. "You've just got bits of metal to fight with.

"I've come in the name of the mighty God of Israel."

He fitted a stone in his sling, whirled it around, and...

The stone hit Goliath, who fell down with a thump.
  David had WON! He had WON!
  David had expected a big day out.
It was the biggest ever.

.......poing

35

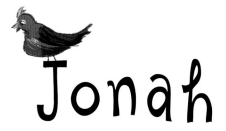

Jonah

Jonah was a prophet. Well, he was supposed to be. He was SUPPOSED to listen to God and then tell people what God had said.

Then one day God said this to him: "Go to Nineveh. The people there are doing the wickedest things. Tell them to stop... or they'll be in deep, dark trouble."

Jonah scowled a deep, dark scowl. He began to think deep, dark thoughts.

"The people of Nineveh deserve to be in trouble," he said to himself.

"I won't go."

He packed his bag and set off in the opposite direction.

He went down to the sea. He got on a boat that was bound for far away.

"If God wants a prophet, God will have to come and find me," he chuckled.

God was watching as the boat set sail. God was watching as Jonah went below deck to sleep. God sent a storm.

W**h**ooo**o**oo went the wind.

CR**A**SH
went the waves.

"Help!"

cried the sailors. "This is such a dreadful storm.

"It can only mean one thing: someone on board has done something dreadful, and their god is trying to punish them."

So they got everyone on deck. They played the choosing game to find out who had done a dreadful thing.

The choosing game pointed to JONAH.

"You villain," the sailors cried. "We're in deepest, darkest trouble, and all because of YOU!"

Jonah drooped his head. "You're right," he mumbled. "I'm running away from God. Throw me overboard."

"No, no," the sailors agreed. "That would be a wicked thing for us to do."

"It's what I want," said Jonah, and he frowned his deep, dark frown.

"Well, in that case..."

wwhooooooooosh

The sailors threw Jonah into the sea.
The wind blew away to a whisper.
The waves settled down to sleep.
And Jonah sank down

down

down.

There at the bottom of the deep, dark sea,

a WHALE came and...

swallowed him up. Whole.

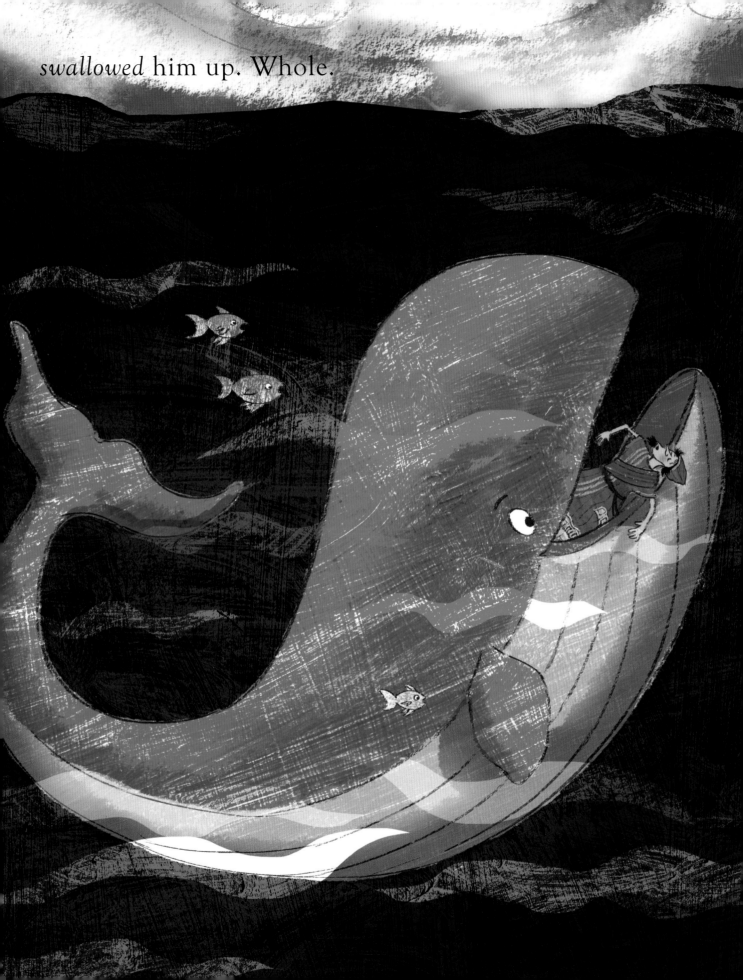

Deep inside the whale, everything was dark. Jonah wiped a tear. It was hard to tell that it was a tear, because everything was so wet, but even so.

"I'm sorry, God," muttered Jonah. "Please help me. I'll do anything you want. Everything you want. Really, honestly."

God heard what Jonah said, which goes to show that trying to run away from God is never going to work. And God told the whale to take Jonah to shore.

burp

Back on shore, Jonah hurried all the way to Nineveh.

"Listen up, you wicked people," he shouted. "God is warning you:

"Stop your wicked ways, or you'll all be in deep, dark trouble."

The people of Nineveh listened. All of them.

"That man's right!" said the king. And he made an announcement:

"People of Nineveh: STOP your wicked ways."

And they did.

Jonah stomped off out of the city. He built a little shelter and watched. Surely God wouldn't let the people of Nineveh off a really gruesome punishment. Surely there would be fire and brimstone or thunder and lightning or SOMETHING.

Nothing.

Jonah frowned. If anything, his frown was getting deeper and darker.

"I knew you'd do that, God," grumbled Jonah. "You go all soft and forgiving even when people have been utterly and completely dreadful.

"And you leave me sitting here melting in the sun."

God heard Jonah. God woke a seed and a lovely green plant grew over the little shelter and shaded it from the sun.

"Lovely," said Jonah.

Then God woke a worm, and the worm ate the stem and the plant died.

"My poor plant!" wailed Jonah. "Honestly, God, you can be so unfair!"

"Do you think so?" asked God. "You can feel sorry for a plant, but I'm not supposed to be sad when people get things all messed up.

"I really care about Nineveh: the people, the children, and all the animals."

Daniel

KING DARIUS LEANED back on his throne and sighed. It was THOSE men again.

"King Darius, may you live for ever," they said, and they bowed low.

King Darius rolled his eyes to the heavens. With men like these pestering him, even a quiet afternoon *felt* like for ever.

"You know Daniel," said the men.

"Yes," said the king. "Good man. I trust him."

"Well," said the men. "There's a problem.

"You made a law not long ago saying no one could appeal for anything from anyone but you."

"Oh yes," said the king. "That was your idea. Not the worst you've had."

"O great and wonderful king," said the men, "it is YOUR great and wonderful law, and therefore cannot be broken.

"The trouble is... Daniel has broken it.

"We've seen him saying prayers to his God.

"It seems he thinks God is rather more important than you."

"Oh well," said Darius. "That's just Daniel.

"He's good through and through. I don't mind a bit."

The men crept closer.

"But the *LAW*," they said. "YOUR LAW.

"You can't have just anyone breaking the *LAW*. He must be punished according to the *LAW*.

"And you know what that means...

"You must have him THROWN TO THE LIONS."

50

King Darius was very upset. For one long dark night he paced up and down. He could think of nothing but Daniel.

No, he didn't want dinner.

No, he didn't want music.

No, he did NOT want a helpful servant asking him if there was anything to be done that would help.

At this rate, the king was not just going to live for ever. He was going to be awake for ever.

The next day dawned. King Darius hurried to the lions' den.

"Daniel," he called in a little trembling voice.

"Good morning, Your Majesty," came the cheerful reply.

"I'm not sure you were expecting to see me this morning.

"But I'm perfectly fine.

"My God is rather special, you see. My God heard my prayers and sent an angel to keep me safe."

ZZ...ZZZ

King Darius was overjoyed. "Pull that man to safety at ONCE," he ordered his soldiers.

"Everyone needs to know about Daniel's great and wonderful God, who is deserving of the highest praise.

"And as for those people who didn't want anyone saying prayers to that God... "I have the punishment waiting hungrily."

54

ROARRRR

GROWL

Baby Jesus

THE PEOPLE OF Nazareth had gathered in the marketplace.

"There's going to be a big announcement," they whispered. "From the emperor in Rome."

"I can guess," said an old man. "He'll be wanting us to pay more tax money so he can have a bigger palace. I'll eat my sandals if that's not it."

That made Mary smile.

The old man was right. Everyone had to go to their home town to put their name on the list of taxpayers.

"And as we're going to be married," said Joseph to Mary, "you and I will have to go together to my home town of Bethlehem."

"Don't you mind that I am expecting a baby?" asked Mary.

"No, I don't," replied Joseph. "An angel spoke to you and an angel spoke to me. Your baby is God's special baby. And I'm going to take care of you both."

That made Mary smile.

Together Mary and Joseph made the long journey to Bethlehem.

So did a lot of other people whose home town was Bethlehem.

And that's why, when Mary and Joseph arrived, there was no room left in the inn.

Instead, they had to shelter in a stable.

Never mind the ox.

mooooo

squea

eeyore Never mind the donkey.

Never mind the sheep and
the goats and the chickens...

cluck

And doesn't every stable have mice?
"I think the baby will be born very soon," said Mary.
"I don't mind."
And still she smiled.

Out on the hillside nearby, some shepherds were watching their sheep.
Suddenly, from a burst of light, an angel spoke.

"Good news!

The best of news. News to make this dark world bright!"

"You've already done that," muttered a shepherd grumpily.

"Tonight," said the angel, "a baby has been born in Bethlehem. He is the one who will bring God's blessing to all the world!"

The shepherds went... and they saw.

There in a stable they found Mary and Joseph and the newborn baby Jesus.

Mary listened to the tale the shepherds told, and she smiled.

sparkle

"You're a very special boy," she said, as she rocked the little baby Jesus. "Look at that star. It's shining right above this house. It's like it's shining just for you."

And it seems that Mary was right, for the light of that same star led wise men to Bethlehem.

They brought rich gifts: gold, frankincense, and myrrh.

"Gifts for a king," they said.

And Mary smiled.

The storm at sea

WHEREVER JESUS WENT, crowds came to listen to him.

"It's not a bother," he told his friends. "It's what I'm meant to be doing with my life.

"But I have done enough talking in the place we came to today.

"Tomorrow, let's go somewhere else."

They walked down to the shore of Lake Galilee, and their boat.

"I'll be captain," said the friend named Peter. (He was a fisherman, after all. In fact, it was because of him that they HAD a boat.)

"Or I could be captain," said his brother Andrew. He was a fisherman too.

"And I'm a fisherman," said James.

"Me too," said James's brother.

"I don't want a squabble about who's going to be captain," sighed Jesus. "I want a lie-down."

He got on the boat and found a pillow. He shut his eyes and let his friends get on with the sailing.

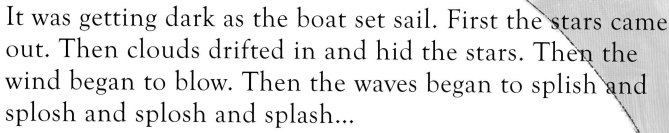

It was getting dark as the boat set sail. First the stars came out. Then clouds drifted in and hid the stars. Then the wind began to blow. Then the waves began to splish and splosh and splosh and splash...

And CRASH and SMASH and...

Scary!

"Help!" cried some and
"DON'T PANIC," ordered Andrew.
"Don't you go telling people what to do," shouted Peter.
"I'm the captain and I say...

"ALL HANDS ON DECK!"

"That means get bailing," muttered James.

"I'll wake Jesus," said John.

He shook Jesus awake. "Wake up! Help us!" he said. "Or we'll all drown!"

Jesus stood up in the boat.
He looked at the storm. Then...
"Be still," he said to the wind.
"Lie down," he said to the waves.

69

All at once, the sea was still.
"Why were you frightened?" he asked his friends.

"Have you no faith?"

He sat down and appeared to doze off. The friends began to whisper.

"Odd."

"Scary."

"Who can Jesus really be?"

"Even the wind and waves obey him."

The hole
in the roof

JESUS WAS SITTING on a chair, talking, talking, talking.

He talked about this, he talked about that, but mainly he talked about God.

"Make it your aim to live as God wants," he told his listeners. "Love one another, as God loves you. Forgive one another, and God will forgive you."

Among the listeners was a row of frowning men. "You're just a carpenter from Nazareth!" they grumbled. "What do you know about God? We've spent years studying the holy books and we're a bit wiser than you."

They would have gone on grumbling, but something was happening that made everyone think about something else.

Why were bits of the ceiling falling down around them?

There appeared to be some kind of hole.

It was growing...

And growing...

And then, to everyone's astonishment, a man was lowered down right in front of Jesus.

On the flat roof above, four men waved and grinned.

The owner of the house shook his fist. "Why did you do that?" he cried.

"We can't get through the door," came the answer. "There are crowds trying to get in."

Jesus looked at the man. He was lying on a sleeping mat. He pointed to his legs.

"Can't walk," he muttered.

"You can still be cheerful," said Jesus. "All the wrong you have ever done is forgiven."

"Tut tut TUT!"

complained the grumbly old men.

"You're not allowed to say such things.

Only GOD can forgive."

Jesus shrugged. "It was an easy thing to say," he said. "I could have said to this man, 'Get up and walk,' but only God can work miracles.

"After all, if I did say that and it worked... well, everyone would see that God backs what I say."

He turned to look at the man on the mat.
"Here's another reason to be cheerful," said Jesus.

"Get up and walk."

To everyone's amazement, he did.
So what were the grumbly men to make of that!

The good Samaritan

THE MAN HURRYING along looked very pleased with himself.

"I have a clever question," he said to himself. "It's sure to catch Jesus out. It will prove that when he talks about God, he doesn't know what he's talking about.

So he went up to Jesus and asked:

"What must I do to please God?"

Jesus smiled. "I can see you're a man who has studied the holy books. What do they say about the matter?"

"Ah, that's easy," said the man. He was very proud of his learning. "You must love God with all your being, and love your neighbour as yourself."

"Quite right," said Jesus. "There's your answer."

The man felt angry. His trick question hadn't worked. Quickly he thought of another.

"The problem is," he went on, "who is my neighbour?"

Jesus told a story.

"There was once a man who was going from Jerusalem to Jericho.

"As he walked the long and lonely road, robbers sprang out from their hiding places.

BASH

BIFF

"They knocked him down. They beat him up. They took all he had and ran away.

"They left him for DEAD.

"It so happened that another man was making the same journey: a priest from the Temple in Jerusalem.
  "He saw the man lying in the road.

"Then he hurried by

on the other side.

"But never fear – there was another man making the same journey: a helper from the Temple in Jerusalem.

"He saw the man lying in the road. He looked around nervously. Something bad had happened, and here he was, all alone in the bad place. Whatever should he do?

"He walked up to the man. Oh dear. Whatever had happened was REALLY bad.

"He hurried on by.

"Then another man came along. This one was a Samaritan."

Well, no one would expect help from Samaritans. They were a bunch of foreigners with funny ideas about everything. Samaritans wouldn't go to the Temple in Jerusalem even for sightseeing!

"The Samaritan stopped," said Jesus. "He went over to the man and bandaged his wounds.

"He lifted him onto his donkey and took him to an inn, where he took good care of him.

"In the morning, the Samaritan had to travel on. He went to the innkeeper and gave him two coins.

"'Please take care of the man I brought here yesterday,' he said. 'If you spend more, I'll pay the extra next time I'm here.'"

clink
clink

Jesus looked up at the man who had come with a question.

"Now tell me," he said. "Which of the passers-by was a neighbour to the man in need?"

"The one who was kind to him," came the answer.

"Exactly," said Jesus. "Do you want to live in a way that pleases God? Then you go and do the same."

The lost sheep

BAA

BAA

WHEREVER JESUS WENT, crowds would come to listen to his stories.

Whenever Jesus was telling stories to the crowds, others would come to grumble and sneer.

"That Jesus isn't up to much," they would say. "Just look at the kind of people who think he's wonderful. Decent people wouldn't even say hello to them.

"Jesus welcomes them all.

"How dare he talk about right and wrong! He knows nothing."

Jesus told a story.

"There was once a shepherd who had a hundred sheep. He knew each and every one.

"So of course, he noticed when one went missing. Of course, he was upset.

"He left the flock of ninety-nine safe in the pasture.

  "Up the steep and stony track, and faraway over the hills, he went looking for his lost sheep.

  "He clambered over rocks. He squeezed past thorn bushes. He shook his stick at prowling animals.

growwwl

GRRRRR

SSSSS S S SSSSS

93

"At long long last he found it.
   "He picked it up and carried it home.
   "Then he called to his neighbours.
   "'I found my lost sheep! Let's have a party to celebrate.'"

HURRAH

BLEAT

tra la la

tra la la

"God is like that shepherd," said Jesus.
"God notices the people who go astray.
"All heaven sings for joy when they come back home to him."